CATH KIDSTON
COMING UP ROSES

COMING UP ROSES

THE STORY OF GROWING A BUSINESS
Cath Kidston with Sue Chidler

Quadrille
PUBLISHING

This book is for everyone who has been part of the 'CK' journey and, above all, for Hugh and Jo for all their support – it wouldn't have been possible without you.

Many thanks to Sue Chidler in particular, who has been so instrumental in this project. Thanks also to Elisabeth Lester, Pia Tryde, Elaine Ashton, Julie Anglesio, Andy Luckett, Louise Rainey, Jody Kerr and Paula Boyce; to Luke Powell and Claudia Doms of Hudson-Powell and all the team at Quadrille.

Editorial director: Anne Furniss
Art director: Helen Lewis
Creative concept & original text: Sue Chidler
Research editor & archivist for Cath Kidston: Elisabeth Lester
Book design: Hudson-Powell
Copy editor: Zelda Turner
Picture research: Katie Horwich
Production: Aysun Hughes, Vincent Smith

First published in 2013 by
Quadrille Publishing Limited
Alhambra House
27–31 Charing Cross Road
London WC2H 0LS

Cataloguing-in-Publication Data: a catalogue record for this book is available from the British Library.

ISBN 978 184949 250 8
Printed and bound in China

CONTENTS

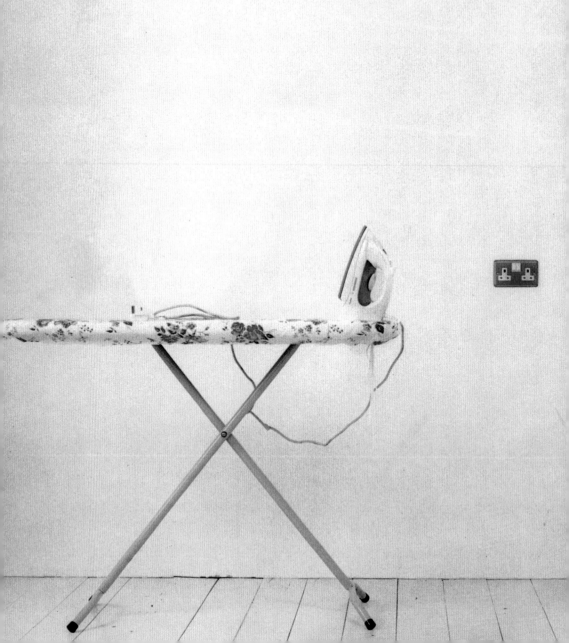

London, 2012

When I set up Cath Kidston in a small shop in Holland Park in 1993 I had no idea what a journey the company would take me on. Besides needing to make a living I had just one ambition: to sell practical, cheerful products for the home with a distinctive modern vintage look. I felt confident there was a gap in the market but I never dreamt the business would grow to the size it is today.

The question I am most frequently asked is how the company evolved from having one employee into what is now a global brand. It really has been a case of taking it one step at a time and learning from my mistakes. Some of the best decisions have been happy accidents, others the result of serious focus and planning. It has taken a lot of hard work and tenacity but this has been driven by a blind belief in the original concept and a lot of support from the people around me.

When we came to make a book to celebrate the company's 20th birthday it seemed appropriate to tell the story of how the business has grown. We have received so much correspondence over the years from enterprising people who are starting up or running their own companies and I wanted to share my experience (both good and bad) to give a little insight into what it took to get the business to where it is today.

Cath Kidston may have changed beyond all recognition but the original inspiration for the company seems as relevant as ever. I feel so lucky to have enjoyed the success I have had but above all I am grateful to be able to come to work every day and still be involved in something I love.

Cath Kidston

GROWING UP

'I don't think any of my family or friends would have predicted that I'd run my own business or be considered a successful entrepreneur. With my upbringing, there just wasn't that kind of expectation of me growing up. But look a little deeper and I think that you can see all the ingredients and inspiration for what was to come.'

Born on 6 November 1958, Cath Kidston looks back at her English country childhood with great nostalgia. 'I spent most of my time outdoors and played a lot with my older sister Janie, my younger brothers Geordie and Hugo, and our vast collection of pets – dogs, rabbits, goldfish, hamsters, birds, even a couple of rescued donkeys. It was a very happy childhood. We grew up in a lovely Georgian house in Hampshire, and Beauty the donkey would often come into our sitting room when we were having tea. To us it was perfectly normal but I imagine others may have found it slightly eccentric!

'I have an incredibly visual memory and can vividly recall all the colours and prints and fabrics of my childhood home. I can still picture my bedroom with its pale blue walls and striped rosebud curtains, the overblown chintz in our playroom, the coloured formica worktops and gloss paint. My sister and I would keep one another entertained for hours, making things and rearranging the furniture in our room. If we ever complained that we had nothing to do, my mother would say, "It's the bore who makes life boring", so we learnt pretty early on how to keep ourselves busy.

MY MOTHER WOULD SAY, 'IT'S THE BORE WHO MAKES LIFE BORING!'

'Our father Archie wanted us to be well-read and curious about the world and to think for ourselves. Our mother Susie gave us quite an old-fashioned and traditional childhood, with plenty of time for playing in the garden, riding horses and getting up to mischief. Like many children with time on our hands, we could be rather naughty when left to our own devices, and loved playing practical jokes. I remember concocting a very realistic-looking chocolate cake and presenting it to my parents and their friends. Little did they know it was made from mud...

'We had lots of fun making and baking, and I used to enter all the competitions at our local village fete. I won the prize for best rock cakes one year, though I didn't really deserve the credit. I think I'd given the mixture a stir and licked the spoon – not much of a contribution.

'We watched *Blue Peter* religiously and my highlight of the week was to recreate the projects from the show. I made all sorts of weird and wonderful gifts over the years. I remember wrapping pairs of old beige tights round wooden coat hangers then covering the lot in fabric to make padded hangers. I was so excited to be invited onto *Blue Peter* a few years ago. We made a village from kitchen sponges and I was finally awarded a *Blue Peter* badge. I probably shouldn't say this but I think I was more thrilled by that than when I received my MBE!'

Rather than attending primary school, Cath was sent to the home of Miss Lawson, a lady who lived in the village, who taught several of the local children for a couple of hours

GROWING UP

Photos of me growing up in Hampshire
from our family album.

each day. 'We spent the morning writing – essentially copying passages from books – and quite often Miss Lawson would leave us to it while she went and did her gardening. She didn't notice that I wrote back to front, in a sort of mirror writing, as I could copy the text perfectly. I also had problems reading aloud, but it wasn't until I was in my twenties that I realised I had some form of dyslexia.'

Formal education was a series of boarding schools where Cath spent any free time in the art room with friends. 'I found most of my lessons incredibly dull and took every opportunity to do something more creative. My dyslexia was diagnosed once I started school, but my parents decided not to tell me that anything was amiss as they didn't want me to feel different. It put me at a disadvantage when it came to the written word, but I excelled in English, History, Geography and Art, as I could visualise the bigger picture. Algebra was more of a challenge and I was happy to give up all the sciences at the age of twelve. Biology made me feel physically sick!

'There wasn't too much pressure to be academic. Afternoons were often spent going on nature walks or riding, which I really enjoyed. And although I did come top of my class in Latin and was happy to inform my parents of my achievement, when my father tested me on a very simple Latin phrase, I had to confess that I came top for drawing the best picture of a Roman in a toga. Needless to say, I never returned to that school!

'I made lots of great friends at school and it wasn't an unhappy time, but it felt a bit like treading water, as though life wouldn't begin properly until I left. From a young age, my favourite hobby was playing shop. I liked the idea of earning money and my first "shop" was in a laurel bush using leaves for money. I became a bit more sophisticated as I got older and my best friend and I would take anything we could find at her house – bits of soap, stuff from the larder – and sell it back to her parents and their friends.

CATH'S PETS

Goldfish – Pinky & Perky

Donkeys – Beauty & Bertie

Ponies – Robin & Bimbo

Hamster – Peanut

Parrot – Beetle

Rabbit – Cottontail

Dogs – Woollie, Emma, Rufus,
Lucy, Shoo Shoo, Albie, Joan

Tortoise – Slowcoach

Budgie – Joey

I can't say I was a born trader, but I loved
the thrill of selling from an early age, even
if it was only my aunt's vegetables!

16

'Our home in Hampshire was fairly isolated, which meant there wasn't a lot of passing trade, so I loved visiting my cousins on the Isle of Wight as their house was on a busy street with lots of potential customers walking by. One day we dug up the entire contents of my aunt's vegetable garden, laid it all out on trays and set up a stall on the pavement outside the house. I sold the mostly unripe veg to passers-by for the sum total of one pound. My aunt was furious, and we were made to send the profits to the RSPCA, but I remember how thrilled I was that I'd been able to persuade someone to buy something from me. I think that's when I got the true bug for shops and shopping. My friend even claims that I said one day I wanted to see my name in lights over a shop door.

'As a teenager, I still loved selling, but I took great pleasure in shopping too. Growing up in the country, most of my clothes came on approval through the post, so my biggest thrill was going to buy stationery at the local shop. And at the village fete, there was always a white elephant stall, which I would scour for a bargain. I loved the sense of anticipation, the not knowing what I might find – it was a treasure trove for me. I guess it was the childhood equivalent of a car boot sale, which I still love today!

'To earn some money, I got a couple of part-time jobs. Aged fifteen, I cleaned the honeymoon suite at the Hare & Hounds and the following year, I cleaned a house on Wednesday afternoons, cycling to work in Sevenoaks while the other girls were playing lacrosse at school. I remember shagpile carpet was all the rage back then and I was always in such a dilemma as to which way to hoover the pile – in stripes or diagonally.

'I studied my A-levels at West Heath – chosen because we were allowed to smoke there, not because of its academic record! And despite all my extracurricular activities, I passed three A-levels in Art, History of Art and English Literature, and won prizes in Art. But by the time I was seventeen, I was ready to leave school behind me and make my own choices – both good and bad. I was always pretty headstrong and felt very grown up at that age. I was keen to ditch the kilts and the Shetland jumpers and have fun with my sister, who was already living in London.

'My mother had worked in a series of shops before she got married so I suppose she assumed I would do the same. She considered it a positive disadvantage for a girl to be a well-educated "blue-stocking" and certainly didn't believe in girls going to university. I'm not sure what my parents really expected of me apart from that I would get married in due course and become a housewife and a mother. I just had to earn some kind of living in the meantime.

WHY WOULD I CHOOSE TO DO MORE EXAMS WHEN I COULD BE EARNING MY OWN MONEY?

'I was at a bit of a loss as to what to do, but was very clear that I didn't want to waste the next three or four years studying for a degree I had no interest in. Why would I choose to do more exams when I could be earning my own money working in a shop? I didn't have a long-term plan. I was just trying to find my way, like most of my friends back then.'

Though the seeds of commerce were sown in her early childhood – a combination of creativity and ingenuity and a love for buying and selling – it would take another twenty years for Cath to channel her passion and find the right outlet for her talents. In the meantime, she was off to London to find work!

Here I am aged nine, looking very Pony Club,
but riding every afternoon was much more
fun than school.

OFF TO WORK

'Moving to London was exciting and, at the same time, quite daunting. A great group of friends had congregated there – some of us were working, some were still studying, but none of us had any real sense of responsibility. We did all sorts of jobs just to pay the rent, go out, shop and not have to run home to our parents!

'It was much easier to jump from job to job at that time and people were more willing to give a young person a chance, so there wasn't the pressure to stay in a job you didn't like. I tried my hand at pretty much everything – cleaning, walking dogs, working in a gift shop, even packing chocolates in a basement on Sloane Street. In my free time, I visited galleries and made the most of the fantastic shops around London. I have always been very visual and where I lacked creative opportunities in my work, I looked for other outlets. I'd go to Brick Lane or charity shops hunting for items that I could customise. I didn't have a proper place of my own at that time, so I spent most of my money on clothes.'

A photo of me (right) doing my first
and last ever modelling job!

Cath's favourite place to shop was Kensington Market as it was a real mecca for second-hand, customised and alternative clothing. 'It was like walking into another world with so much choice. It was dark and exciting with lots of stalls selling quite outrageous clothes. I suppose I was a bit hippyish back then so I'd save up for a pair of loons or be lusting after an Afghan coat with an amazing silk floral lining. If I couldn't afford a Forbidden Fruits frock, I'd search for a second-hand floral tea dress that I could cut up and alter.

'My taste was probably a backlash against the type of outfits my mother had dressed me in. Like most parents of her generation, she bought me clothes that felt very formal and old-fashioned. Every once in a while she would get me something that I liked from a boutique on Sloane Square, but I was keen to make my own money so that I could shop in Miss Selfridge or buy shoes from Ravel. My favourite shop at the time was Fiorucci. I'd pair my Fiorucci velvet trousers with a Fiorucci cherub t-shirt or an angora jumper, accessorised with a pair of yellow suede shoes I'd bought in the sale for £10 from Manolo Blahnik's first shop. Yellow suede – and I wondered why they were in the sale! But I thought I was the epitome of style in that outfit.

IT WAS LIKE WALKING INTO ANOTHER WORLD WITH SO MUCH CHOICE

'It was a wonderfully carefree time and, with hindsight, I was learning by a process of elimination who inspired me and what kind of work I was drawn to. No matter what job I did, I was always trying to find something that I could make and sell, but I just didn't know how to make my ideas commercial. And even if I had hit on the perfect idea at that time, I was rather shy and unsure of myself and didn't have the self-confidence to make it a success.

'One of my early money-spinning ideas was making old-school-style shirts from Airtex cotton. I remember buying yards of Airtex to make the shirts, but then realising that I would never make a profit, so the Airtex just sat there.

NO PARKING

CELLY BUSTER

↑ KITCHEN

HOME M...

BEEFBURGERS

TOASTED

SANDWICHES

AND

DRINKS

NO DOGS ALLOWED

← TAKE - AWAY SANDWICHES AND DRINKS

...ACKS ...NDWICHES DRINKS

↓

KENSINGTON MARKET   BAR

ANOT... 40 ST... IN THE B...

TO BELLY BUSTER CAF...

The retail price would have been out of this world for such a basic garment if I'd tried to make a proper margin. Although I didn't appreciate it at the time, that taught me a very valuable lesson in business economics.

'I also worked as a freelance window dresser for Laura Ashley. I knew the Ashley family as they were neighbours of ours in Wales and on one occasion Laura's daughter Jane had asked me to model with her and a few other friends for their catalogue. I've always hated having my photograph taken, so I was under no illusion that I'd found my vocation. But working in shops was much more my thing. I just loved selling, talking with customers, organising the rails and rearranging the windows. I guess the staff discount helped as well!

'London was very exciting, but then, when I was nineteen, my father died from a brain tumour. It was utterly unexpected and a shock for the whole family. Dad was just fifty and he had been the centrifugal force in our family. It was like having the rug pulled out from under us.

'My brothers were still relatively young, at eleven and thirteen years old. My mother was only forty-eight and went from being the stereotypical wealthy housewife, who had never had to work, to looking after my two younger brothers, the house, worrying about money and having to make all the decisions on her own. I never heard Mum complain about how things had turned out for her following my father's death. I was very proud of how well she adapted to such a change in circumstances; she coped remarkably. But I decided that I never wanted to find myself in that situation; I vowed to be independent and take care of myself.

'It's said that it takes about seven years to truly come to terms with the loss of a parent or spouse, to restabilise. I think this certainly applied to me after my father died. At the funeral, I remember thinking that I'd have to show him what I could do to make him proud. As for anyone who loses a parent at an early age, the experience changed me.'

CATH'S JOBS

Playing shop

Cleaner at the Hare & Hounds

Domestic cleaner

Laura Ashley model

Bendicks chocolate packer

Dog walker

Temp at the Science Museum

Gift shop attendant

Gallery assistant

Picture framer

Freelance window dresser

Clothes shop assistant

Assistant to antique textiles dealer

Apprenticeship at Nicky Haslam

Interior designer

Curtain shop owner

Owner of Cath Kidston Ltd

Cath put a renewed focus into finding a career that she could stick with and set about making her first flat in London into a proper home. 'I lived in a very small flat but was forever rearranging the furniture, just like I had as a child. My best friend and I used to sit for hours describing our imaginary house of the future and how we would decorate each room, from the furniture to the colours.

'I started a City and Guilds Art course but left after a term as I missed having an income. By this stage, I was keen to gain more practical experience and started helping friends with their various entrepreneurial projects. In 1978 you either went punk or New Romantic. I was definitely more drawn to a frilly shirt, so when my cousin wanted to get a business off the ground selling Lady Diana-style pie crust shirts, I tagged along with her to the East End factory where they were being made. I loved feeling a part of things, although I was probably just the annoying little cousin trying to help!

'I also began collecting what I would call "kitchenalia" – bits from junk shops and vintage fabric – thinking about the homes I might have and how I could use all these bargain finds. I was probably inspired by childhood trips with my grandmother and aunt to some wonderful furniture and fabric stores. My father's side of the family loved interiors and I had always admired my Granny's style.

'Friends started asking for help or advice on their own decorating projects. I was a free pair of hands and they seemed to trust my eye. And when someone I knew left her job with Joss Graham, a dealer in antique textiles, I fell into that role almost by accident and suddenly got a sense of what I might do in life. I've always had an almost photographic memory for prints; they have such strong associations for me, especially of childhood memories. So to earn a living dealing with things I loved was hugely appealing.'

With no formal qualifications and practically no on-the-job experience, Cath found it hard to fathom her next step into the interior design world. 'I hadn't grown up in an arty family, but I took inspiration from my cousin Belinda Bellville, who was very successful at the time as one half of the fashion label Bellville Sassoon. Belinda had such wonderful natural style. She was always very encouraging to me and suggested that I pursue something creative.

'Not knowing how else to go about things, I drew up a list of interior designers I admired and set about contacting them over the next twelve months, going for interviews and networking, looking for any opportunity to get my career started. It was going to require someone to take quite a leap of faith to give me a chance. Nothing happened for a year, but then a friend of mine who had a shop round the corner from Nicky Haslam sort of introduced us and encouraged me to meet with him.'

I WAS SENT ON MY OWN TO MEASURE UP CURTAINS FOR AVA GARDNER. IT WAS THE FIRST TIME I'D REALLY LOVED MY JOB

During the 1980s, Nicky Haslam was one of London's most famous interior designers, renowned for his work with celebrities, royals, musicians and movie stars. Spotting something special in the twenty-five-year-old Cath, he gave her a week's trial, which turned into four years at the interiors company, during which everything started to fall into place. 'I started right at the bottom and did anything and everything that was asked of me, including walking Nicky's dog. Gradually he gave me more and more responsibility.

'It was exciting accompanying Nicky on client visits, meeting famous people and seeing inside their houses. I'd only just started working for him when I was sent all on my own to measure up curtains for Ava Gardner. It was the first time I'd really loved my job. It seemed so glamorous – even if I was only there with my tape measure. But what I liked most was getting all the fabric samples and trimmings and putting them all together.

My garden flat in Hammersmith was featured
in World of Interiors just as I launched the
business. It was fortunate PR.

The flat was full of antique
fabrics and car boot finds.

'I learnt an awful lot during those years. It was the first time that I'd really stuck at anything and, thanks to Nicky, I started to believe that I had an eye for colour and print, for combining fabrics and texture. The job also introduced me to a whole new world of clients and contacts, interior design journalists and editors. It all helped build my confidence, and after four years I was ready to develop my own ideas. I had £5,000 saved and, alongside the decorating work, I really wanted to open a shop, but I wasn't quite brave enough to go it alone. I was looking for the support of a business partner.'

Her friend Shona McKinney had the same ambitions. 'It was the late 1980s, and swags and tails and really grand curtains were in vogue. Shona and I both wanted to do something on our own and we saw a gap in the market. Curtains had become serious – a real focal point in the room – the more ornate, the better. And I had an idea for a shop that would be all things curtain related; there wasn't really another store specialising like that.'

In 1987, the two friends became equal business partners, both investing £5,000 in McKinney Kidston, and opening their tiny curtain shop on Walton Street, just off the King's Road. Cath was twenty-nine. 'Our closest competitors in Chelsea were Peter Jones and Harrods, both of which seemed a bit old and stuffy. Shona and I offered something fresh and designed everything to a customer's specifications.

'The shop was a veritable Aladdin's cave. Around half of the business was old vintage stock, such as curtain poles and finials, and the other half was vintage textiles. Shona ran most of the business side of things and was very organised, while I did a lot of the buying and the interior design work. At that time, if you wanted help from an interior designer, your only option was to have a whole room redecorated. We offered that service, but we were also happy to simply advise on all things curtain related. That was our point of difference.

'There were so many new challenges to the role: I was learning how to source and bidding at auctions for stock. I was managing people, finding suppliers who could make things to my design, balancing the accounts, buying textiles. We worked with vintage fabrics but we also played a lot with colour tones, dipping fabrics in tea or instant coffee to get just the right aged shade. To advertise our products, we produced a big catalogue for the trade, using a combination of line drawings and photographs. Then the press picked up on the concept and our tiny shop gained quite a reputation, featuring regularly in magazines such as *World of Interiors* and *House and Garden*.'

As testament to the strength of the original idea and the business the two women built together, the shop continues to thrive today under the trading name McKinney & Co. But after four years, Cath was ready to break out. In 1992 she sold her share in the business to Shona and the partnership was dissolved. 'I had taken "curtainalia" as far as I could. It was time for something different and I started to think of new ideas for a shop that I could run alone.'

Our tiny shop was an Aladdin's cave of
'curtainalia', tapping into the trend for
over the top curtains.

THE EUREKA MOMENT

'Flicking through a magazine one day, I saw a photo of a bathroom that was so simple and uncluttered. I loved the old rose wallpaper on the side of the bath, the glossy paint on the big armoire. It summed up all the ideas I'd had about using English heritage designs and giving them a twist. It was my eureka moment!

'I'd given a lot of thought to what I should do next, what the concept could be. I had no interest in trying to copy something that was already out there, but I still wanted to sell and interact with customers, so I knew I should have some kind of shop. I didn't want to compete with an established business – not with the budget I had – so I needed an original idea or a different angle.

'If you think back to the early nineties, they were interesting years politically and socially. The country was just emerging from a recession; New Labour were about to come to power with a young prime minister and there seemed to be a notice-able change in the country's mood – a more relaxed attitude in general. After yuppies and nouvelle cuisine, a more laidback, kitchen supper approach was emerging. Showing off wasn't fashionable any more. Society was changing and my instinct told me that our attitude to decorating was changing too.

'I didn't rush into going solo. I was making a decent enough living with my interior decorating work and the success of McKinney Kidston gave me some thinking time. One of my early ideas was to have a wallpaper shop, which would look like an old-fashioned hardware store. I would have all the wallpaper designed and produced and I imagined the men working there, wearing long aprons, with pencils tucked behind their ears. I saw it as a down-to-earth place in contrast to the really frou-frou decorating shops around.

'I felt sure that some combination of old and new would resonate with people. Car boot sales were starting to spring up and I spent my weekends trawling through heaps of junk. I was looking for lost treasure, for bargains that I could renovate and bring up to date. I loved the anticipation of it all. It took me back to the excitement I'd felt as a child shopping at the white elephant stall at the village fete. And I guessed that if I loved doing this, then there must be others who wanted these reclaimed, restored bits and pieces, but either didn't have the time or the eye to do it themselves.

'During the week, I walked my dog in Shepherd's Bush and every day we'd pass a house clearance shop called Great Expectations. Old painted wardrobes were put outside on the pavement with scratches gouged into them to show the pine underneath. The idea was that people would buy the wardrobes and remove the paint, as stripped pine was a big trend at the time. But I loved the gloss paint.

'I started to think about how I could use cheap, old furniture in a more modern and relevant way. There was a lot of sameness in interiors at the time. All the styles on offer felt very tired and dated. I recognised that there must be a market for something other than the big, brown, antique furniture of my parents' generation and the Scandinavian minimalism that was meant to appeal to my friends and me.

'That magazine bathroom was just what I had in mind. It looked affordable, fresh and fun. I could suddenly visualise a cool junk shop filled with vintage stuff from my car boot sales and the renovated furniture from the house clearance shop, all given a modern makeover.'

Gradually Cath started to build a portfolio of ideas and buy stock with her future shop in mind. 'Alongside the vintage fabric, I amassed a lot of old china and glassware, including a great selection of heavy-cut glass ashtrays in vibrant colours. I bought sets of Redouté rose prints and put them in lighter, more contemporary frames. At that time, all the vintage stuff I sourced was available in abundance, simple to update and, most importantly, cheap to buy.

'I was very influenced by Swedish interiors – not the minimalist approach but simple, old, almost utilitarian furniture. I would buy a wooden table, paint it and put a zinc top on it. I wanted to take all this old-fashioned junk and make it look younger and fresher. The idea tapped into the zeitgeist, albeit a little ahead of its time, but having the experience of making McKinney Kidston a success gave me the confidence to recognise a good marketable concept and turn it into something commercially viable. With hindsight I could say that we kick-started the whole trend. The idea for modern vintage was born!'

YOU ARE
CATH KID
8 CLAREND
SHOP C
WEDNESDAY 9
12 AM
RSVP
TEL071 221 40c

VITED TO

STON LTD

N CROSS WII

PENING

PTEMBER 15TH

O 8PM

FAX

071 229 1992

TEL: 0171 221 4000   FAX: 0171 229 1992

Cath Kidston Ltd

8 Clarendon Cross, London W11 4AP

GETTING STARTED

'Now that I had the concept, I needed to find the right spot for my shop. I needed the rent to be affordable, which meant finding somewhere slightly off the beaten track. But I also wanted a location that had that villagey kind of feel.

'I settled on a tiny store in Clarendon Cross, nestled between Holland Park and Notting Hill. This was before Notting Hill became trendy, but the area had an arty, creative vibe and was starting to attract other small, eclectic businesses. And the annual rent was only £8,000 compared to an average rent of £16,000 in the more established parts of town.

'There was a good space at street level for the shop and a decent-sized basement that I could use for storage. There was also room for me to continue doing interior design projects, to help make ends meet. I wanted to get trading as quickly as possible, but it took around three months to get off the ground. And since I didn't want to risk losing the contacts I'd built up at McKinney Kidston I worked from the basement of the shop during the renovations, with the builders working around me!

'I founded Cath Kidston Ltd in 1993 and even though I felt confident about my idea to combine traditional homeware with a modern twist, opening the first shop felt like quite a risk as there was nothing else like it at that time.

'My budget was only £15,000 and the store needed some money spending on it. It had previously been a tile shop so I had to rip up the old tiled floor and replace it with red lino. A till table needed to be built and I had to design the shop front too. I decided to have the front repainted pale blue and a new black awning was put up with the logo and lettering – all for the sum of £2,000. I wanted us to look like a chic house clearance store. Initially I wasn't going to use my name and thought of simply calling the shop "Household Effects", but we ended up using Cath Kidston because I wanted old clients to be able to find me again and for that I needed to have my name listed in the telephone directory. I still liked Household Effects as a descriptor for the store, and it appeared originally on the awning, but I realised that it probably didn't describe what we were selling when a gentleman came in and asked if he could buy a strimmer!'

Cath employed her cousin Polly to work in the shop and, keen to put all the right building blocks for the business in place, called on her accountant, Jeffrey Cooper, who had helped her negotiate the end of the McKinney Kidston partnership. 'I had a real fear of getting into debt and didn't feel confident enough around the financial side of the business to manage it alone. Although I'm very good at spotting numbers in red on a spreadsheet, one of the first things I did was get the right people in to help me. I knew I could trust Jeffrey to look after the accounts and he appointed a great bookkeeper, Mehmet. I've always had a very simple financial philosophy, which is, "more in than out". I knew that if I kept this in mind, I wouldn't go wrong.

'In order for the business to appear bigger and more professional than it really was, I spent a significant amount of the opening budget on unexciting office equipment. I bought a really expensive, high-quality inkjet printer, one of the early Mac computers and a fax machine. I wanted all my communication and mail-outs to be of a high standard. In order to save money on the more day-to-day operations, I settled for a second-hand till and used old-fashioned invoice books with carbon paper. Customers were given handwritten receipts.

'I filled the shop with beautiful vintage fabric, all the bits and pieces I'd collected at flea markets and car boot sales, and the brightly painted old furniture. Sometimes the freelancers I hired to re-upholster and repaint the chairs and cupboards would work on the pavement outside – we were lucky the shop had a canopy for when it rained! I also invested £3,000 in my first print design: the Rose Bouquet wallpaper, inspired by a wonderful, traditional rose print I had seen in Wales.

'Not long after opening, I began creating my own products. Just a few cushion covers, cotton bags and a flowery ironing board cover to start, all made up in vintage fabric. I lived in a small flat at the time and my ironing board hung on the back of the kitchen door, as that was the only place it would fit. It had the standard silver cover (in the early nineties, it was either silver or a Chippendale-style man in boxer shorts) and one day I just thought, wouldn't it be nice to make something that is so dull – both in terms of style and the activity – into something more cheery?

'I had an actress friend called Dot who was also a trained seamstress, and she agreed to make up these basic, everyday items from her sewing room at home in Hammersmith. I'm sure we wouldn't be allowed to retail the ironing board covers

'Rose Bouquet'

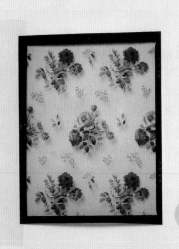

C

C

All. Line Drawings
+ Boxes to be

BLACK + WHITE
~~Throughout~~.

This classic 1950's Rose print comes in **Wallpaper**,
fabric + oilcloth. ~~see page~~ . 3. colourways, blue, yellow +
See pages .18-21 for fabric + wallpaper.   white.

~~on
page~~

| TEL | 0171 221 4000 | To order | ← IN RED |
| FAX | 0171 229 1992 | | |

DATE

Pale *pink* GROUND.

PYJAMAS.   £55 DRESSIN   £65 LAUNDRY BA   £14.95

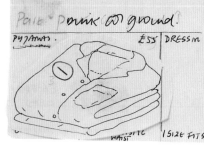

WAIST 27c   1 SIZE FITS M.

TH. 130cm

50 x 85cm.

5

D

D

The Dressing Gown, see here
in yellow, comes in the softest
cotton. and is a generous length
to fit most sizes.

E

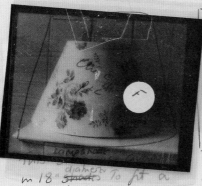

F

in 18" diameter to fit a
larger table lamp.

H

The A4 box files
are covered in the
paper to make the
cheeriest storage!

BLE	£25	LAMPSHADE SUITABLE F TABLE		£38	LAMPSHADE SUITABLE FOR HANGING OR ON TABLE LAMP	£24
4		5			6	
WITH PLTHESITRIM 27×37×7cm.		PAPER COVERED		×29cm×46cm	PAPER COVERED 10×19×30cm	

these days as they would probably fail all fire safety tests, but back then things were far simpler.'

When she wanted to find a manufacturer Cath would rely on the Yellow Pages. 'If only we'd had Google back then! I was learning about sourcing as I went along. I had to ring around to find potential suppliers and then spend hours travelling to visit them at their premises. I worked with small producers, nearly all of them British, whom I could visit, explain

my designs to, and work closely with to develop product in the small quantities I wanted to buy, and could afford. Even if I had been able to find cheaper sources in the Far East, for example, the minimum order quantities I wanted would have been of no interest to the manufacturers.

'I set the retail price based on what I thought I could sell the product for. The small production runs did have a knock-on effect on margins but the more I spent on stock, the tighter the cash flow became. Right from the start, I focused on what I felt represented good value for my customer rather than operating a traditional mark-up strategy. There was no point saying I wanted to make a 65 per cent margin, for example, if this meant the product was unaffordable. Instead, I was prepared to pay myself very little and plough any profit I made back into the business, mainly into stock and keeping the retail prices realistic.'

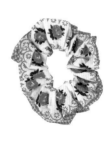

Duvet covers were recycled
into anything from wash bags to my
cousin's swimsuit patterns.

Cath also found one of her key suppliers through a rather unorthodox route. 'Just before opening the shop, I took a holiday with my sister in what was then Czechoslovakia and fell completely in love with this very traditional, brightly coloured rose gingham fabric. Back in London, I approached the Czech embassy and asked them to put me in contact with a fabric supplier. Fortunately for me, my curtain maker Eva was Czech and she acted as translator. I then drove on my own to the factory in east Czechoslovakia – where they also printed army camouflage fabric – and ordered some of the gingham fabric on a roll and some products made up to my designs, including more ironing board covers and some children's bed linen.

'It all worked pretty well for the first order. The fabric was dropped off on a palette outside the shop by a huge van that Polly and I had to unload. Although such was my naivety around importing that I didn't realise I was paying for the pantechnicon to come all the way from eastern Europe! When I placed the second order, however, something must have got lost in translation as instead of receiving 1,500 metres of fabric on a roll, we received the entire quantity already made up as single duvet cover and pillowcase sets. Overnight I became a bed linen heiress!

'I'd tied up a lot of money in that fabric, and the order was non-returnable, so it could have been a disaster. I had to think quickly and decided to cut up the bed linen and make it into smaller items. And with the help of Dot and my new Scottish supplier J & J Walker (whom we still work with today) I created a range of printed products: cushions  and aprons, wash bags, coat hangers, bath hats and frilly fifties-style swimsuits, all designed in the rose gingham fabric. And so my first proper product collection was born... completely by accident!

'Not all successes are down to great planning; sometimes they come out of necessity, as was the case with my rose gingham range. When you're still a very small business, this kind of mistake can be enough to take you down, so it felt almost ironic when the swimsuits were featured in British *Vogue* and *Women's Wear Daily*.

'I was fortunate to receive a lot of positive PR in the early years. I had built up some great relationships with editors and stylists during my time working for Nicky Haslam, and then at McKinney Kidston. And the idea of using vintage fabric on unexpected household items took off immediately. In particular, the floral ironing board cover caught the press's interest. Journalists are always looking for something new to write about and I had a really good piece appear in *World of Interiors* that was picked up by lots of other magazines.

'People started to ring the shop to see if they could buy what they had seen in the articles, and I realised that there was real potential in the mail order side of the business. In response to the demand, I decided to produce a mail order catalogue, but since my budget was so tiny, I used a mixture of line drawings and my own photography to keep costs down.

I'm a terrible photographer but taking my own snaps at home was the only way I could afford to create a catalogue within our budget. I did all the page layouts and copywriting myself, without any kind of computer software. It was all hand made and passed on to the printer in a very cut-and-paste format.'

Cath's first printed products began to gain a fan base, particularly among stylists and prop masters who often called in items to use in photo shoots and films. And it wasn't long before the shop began attracting attention from some high-profile names from the fashion and design worlds. 'Miuccia Prada came into the shop several times and always bought lots of things. And I remember Alexandra Shulman, the editor of British *Vogue*, visited us, as well as other magazine editors and lots of celebrities. I had customers travelling from all over the country just to visit the store. Sometimes they would buy all they needed to decorate an entire room.

Opening my first shop in 1993 was quite a risk as there was nothing else like it at the time.

'Over the next couple of years, we were helped by the fact that Notting Hill was starting to take off. There was a real energy around the place and locals used to love coming into the shop to have a mooch about and a chat. The Post Office was just next door to us, and people would pop in after picking up the child benefit or dropping off a parcel or whatever. At that time you could smoke pretty much wherever you wanted and we would sit in the shop smoking and generally just hanging out.

'Stores such as The Cross and Sumerill & Bishop opened in the neighbourhood and together we made up a lovely enclave. Although I didn't realise it at the time, I guess that we were part of what made this part of West London such an attractive destination.' However, for all the positive press and growing interest, making money from actual sales was proving tough and in its first year of trading the shop turned over only £50,000.

The famous flowery ironing board cover
that caught the attention of the press.

THE EARLY YEARS

'I had a lot of faith in my concept for modern vintage, but many businesses fail in the first couple of years. In spite of all the publicity, the store wasn't yet a commercial success and I was very aware that I couldn't rest on my laurels and expect the business to make money without putting in a lot of effort.

'Cash flow was all important, but having the right amount of stock available without tying up too much working capital was a tricky balancing act. For the vintage side, I was buying stock on a weekly basis at car boot sales, house clearances and markets. For the made-up products, my range of simple, everyday items was limited by what I could afford to order and what could be created in my chosen fabrics.

'Fortunately, Dot was still happy to make up the ironing board and cushion covers with no minimum order. But the manufacturer base who could work to our low quantities and still allow the business to make a margin was limited. The minimum order for wallpaper, for example, was 300 ten metre rolls, which was a big investment for me. The fabric I ordered from Czechoslovakia was inexpensive, but the minimum order for the rose gingham fabric was still 500 metres of each of the three colourways I worked with.

'To help use up the stock, I expanded our product range to include wash bags, tablecloths, lampshades, box files and other useful items. I wanted everything to be beautiful, practical and simple to produce, and the cheery colours and nostalgic prints made them easy purchases, especially as gifts. I also found a factory in the UK that could coat cotton fabric to make oilcloth in fifty-metre runs. It was a key discovery as it meant that I could buy fabric in larger quantities but could bring variety to the products by using it either coated or uncoated.'

Cath's main source of income was still her decorating business, which kept her busy throughout the early nineties. She was attracting lots of interesting clients and being commissioned to design the interiors for everything from flats to country estates to yachts. In her personal life, she also met her now husband, the record producer Hugh Padgham. 'We'd known each other for a number of years, as I'd decorated his house in 1990. At that time, Hugh was a single man in the music industry so I designed his place accordingly. When I moved in, four years later, naturally I had to redesign it to my taste! Trying to juggle a new relationship with a fledgling business wasn't ideal, but we were both so busy with our careers, it actually worked well. Hugh's job as a producer took him away for weeks at a time and my workload was pretty intense, so we never had the luxury of spending a lot of time together, which meant we didn't expect it.

'I was committed to growing my business for the long term and that was reflected in my approach. I was fortunately never short of interiors work, so I used my income from the decorating business to help support the shop, and to develop new designs and products. Money was always tight, but Mehmet, my bookkeeper, would come in once a month to give me a cash flow forecast. If the forecast was gloomy, sometimes I made up the products myself – although

I remember my embarassment one time when a customer came into the shop, picked up a cushion I had sewn and commented on how badly made it was!

'In the early years I worked closely with my accountant Jeffrey to develop a proper business plan. My financial strategy of "more in than out" meant that I didn't expand unless I could fund it and avoided bank loans as I didn't want the stress of owing money. I think it's really important when starting a business to understand the level of risk you're willing to take and the amount of stress you want to put yourself under.

'Minimums continued to be an issue due to the amount of cash tied up in production runs, but I eventually found factories in the UK that would produce smaller print runs. The orders were pricey, so I marked up the fabric by only a small amount in order to grow my customer base and continued to forfeit margin in the hope that it would improve as quantities grew. I always kept the customer at the forefront of my mind – it was about what represented good value to them.

'We did everything we could to keep a tight rein on my finances. However, I do remember one quarter I didn't have enough to pay the VAT bill, so I was lucky to be able to borrow money from Hugh. I made sure I paid him back fairly swiftly! On another occasion, when I was desperate, I sold an archive of inspiration books I'd built up over many years to give myself a quick cash injection.

'I had set out thinking that I would sell through my own store and perhaps my own mail order catalogue, but in order to achieve higher minimum orders I decided to start wholesaling to small boutiques, as well as to large established stores such as Liberty. A number of stores started to approach me to become stockists, because we were getting such positive press coverage. And a girl called Elspeth came into the shop

UNDERSTAND THE LEVEL OF RISK YOU'RE WILLING TO TAKE AND THE AMOUNT OF STRESS YOU WANT TO PUT YOURSELF UNDER

A snap showing the interior of
Clarendon Cross with all the vintage fabric
and some of my own early products.

and asked if I could supply some exclusive items for a number of high-end Japanese stores. In fact, Japanese clients such as Beams, United Arrows and Ships took our products very early on. I remember commissioning some beautiful hand-knitted Shetland wool cardigans for Japan, which were actually made in the Highlands. But I think they must have travelled to us via Shetland pony as they were never, ever on time!'

Realising that wholesale could be a lucrative addition to the business, Cath began to actively court new accounts and exhibited at small trade fairs, such as Top Drawer, in order to gain a wider distribution base. 'It was all a bit of a gamble. Attending trade fairs requires a big outlay without ever guaranteeing you a good return. Added to this, three of my UK fabric printers went under during this time, which meant we had to get hold of the fabric screens and move them to another supplier. It was hard to keep up with demand for some products and on occasion we lost money that had been paid up front. I eventually tried moving some of the production to Northern Ireland, as a factory there was getting grants from the government, so it seemed a safer prospect, but when the Armed Forces contract was given to another firm, the factory's funding was withdrawn and I was back at square one.'

By now, Cath Kidston products were being sold through a number of outlets but these were predominantly in London and the south-east of England, and the press attention on the shop was creating a demand nationwide. 'My sister Janie used to come and help sometimes on Saturdays and would answer the phone. I would often hear her saying to a customer, "Hold the line please and I'll just check if we have that in our warehouse," and then she'd run downstairs to the basement to see if we had the item. I suppose it was a bit smoke and mirrors in the early days, but I thought that people wouldn't take a single girl in a little shop very seriously and I wanted to give the impression of a slick, well-run business that could be trusted. In reality, it was still a very hand-to-mouth existence. If a member of staff didn't turn up I would have to ring round and hope that a friend would help out or we couldn't open the shop if I was away. I remember there were days when we hardly took any money at all in the shop and that was a very unnerving feeling.

'We had a fair few disasters along the way too, such as the time when a customer tripped over my dog who was lying just outside the shop door. She decided to sue and I realised that the dog wasn't covered on the shop insurance, but he was on our home insurance. It paid out quite a bit, I think, as our premiums went through the roof the following year. There was also the awful moment when one of the girls was dressing the window and fell through a dodgy floorboard. Luckily Mike the painter was working in the basement and he caught her. You quickly learn about health and safety!'

In spite of it all, Cath continued to build the business steadily and organically. The Cath Kidston product range grew

I styled and photographed my designs
at home for the early catalogues.

to include more prints, bed linen and key oilcloth products. The number of employees increased from just Cath and Polly to four full-time staff plus a handful of part-timers. Mail order and wholesale started to represent a significant percentage of turnover, and Cath was now producing a regular catalogue that was sent out to several thousand customers.

'With so much going on, I often found myself working a seven day week. From Monday to Friday I was based in the Clarendon shop or travelling for my interior design work, which was extremely time consuming. One of my big projects was decorating a yacht moored in Malta – I travelled there once a month for over a year. Decorating demanded long hours and I would regularly continue working at home in the evenings. I was also still spending my weekends at car boot sales, hunting for stock for the shop. I'd make an early start on Sunday morning then spend the afternoon washing any purchases ready for sale.

'I knew it was all getting too much when I came in to the shop one day and found the door unlocked. I'd been so tired the night before I'd left without locking up!'

ALL OR NOTHING

'In 1995, at the age of thirty-seven, I was diagnosed with breast cancer. When you get a diagnosis like that, you think that life will change in an instant, that your days will suddenly become centred around yoga and green tea. But it took me two years of internal wrestling before I felt able to really focus on what I wanted.

'Going through treatment I knew I couldn't keep running two businesses and spending my weekends sourcing and renovating furniture. We had doubled our turnover at Cath Kidston year on year, but there were still enough troughs in trading to make me nervous. I always had this nagging fear that it could quite easily all come to a halt. When we'd had a particularly quiet week it felt like we'd never have another customer walk through the door again. I think having the fall-back of the design work had become a bit of a habit, rather than a necessity. Trying to divide myself between the shop and my private commissions was a way of hedging my bets, but I realised that this was probably to the detriment of the shop.

'By 1997, Hugh and I had been together for quite a few years, and he was very supportive, so I felt that I had enough security to stop the design work and have the courage of my own convictions. My gut instinct had always told me that my idea would come good, and now was the time.' Cath closed her interior design business and put all her energy into developing her own products and the Cath Kidston brand style. 'It was going to be all or nothing from here on in!'

Almost immediately, Cath landed her first publishing deal for a book entitled *Vintage Style*. 'There was an emerging trend for vintage in fashion, as well as for home, and the publishers wanted me to write a guide to the look and feel I had created in store – the florals, vintage fabrics and soft pastel colours. It was billed as "a return to colour, texture and comfort as an antidote to the recent trend for minimalism". Quite a mouthful, but it summed up what we were after!'

The book received a lot of publicity and brought the concept of modern vintage to a much wider audience. And with Cath's new focus on expanding her product offer, big businesses like Debenhams and Ikea were quick to spot the appeal of her original prints and homewares that resonated with customers who didn't want to live in a pristine white box or their parents' or grandparents' house, but were looking for something fresh and homely.

'Debenhams proposed a Cath Kidston range of bedding and towels that would be marketed under the "Designers at Debenhams" range. It wasn't something that I actively pursued, and there was no big financial reward, but when I was approached with the opportunity to collaborate, I knew that it would help increase awareness of the Cath Kidston brand. Designers at Debenhams was a hugely successful part of their business, which had helped showcase British design talent for a number of years.'

Cath designed two ranges for the department store. The second proved challenging, as Debenhams had a fixed idea of

New products and new prints came
thick and fast once I was totally
focused on the shop.

what they wanted from the brand, which did not sit well with Cath. 'At that point, I realised that it was more important for me to be true to the brand than to produce a range just to take the money and get exposure.

'When I was contacted by Ikea, not long after the Debenhams experience, I was naturally cautious. It would have been easy to be swallowed up by a giant like Ikea. The sense of irony was not lost on me either. Ikea had recently run a huge "Chuck Out Your Chintz" advertising campaign, so I found it interesting that they should want me to design a range of prints for them!

'On the other hand, Ikea are a great barometer of public taste and I knew that if they were successful with florals, it would help kick-start the trend. At a time when I was still trying to establish my own brand, it felt a stretch too far to put my name to the project, but Ikea were happy with that decision. I knew that the money this deal would generate would make a significant difference to the business, so if I could protect the Cath Kidston brand name and get a cash injection, I would have been stupid to say no.

'In the end, Ikea were great to work with and the Rosali print I designed for them was hugely successful. I expected it to be just another print within the Ikea range but I was absolutely amazed when it was an immediate sell-out. Even today there are still people posting on online forums talking about where to get hold of the fabric or curtains, and how it was their most loved print from Ikea.

'Around this time, I was also asked to be part of a design consulting board for Laura Ashley. Collaborating on these different projects gave me an insight into the way businesses of varying scales were organised and how they worked. It made me understand that if I wanted my business to grow, I would need to create my own internal departments.'

Cath took the money she received for the Rosali print rights (in excess of £80,000) and invested it back into her business. 'Alongside the shop, I now had a burgeoning wholesale business, so I moved the company to a separate office in Penzance Place, around the corner from Clarendon Cross; I hired a full-time bookkeeper, took on my first print designer and got someone in to look after mail order. I was starting to put a proper structure in place.'

The Rosali print design I did for Ikea
was one of their bestsellers and gave
my business a big cash injection.

BRAND BUILDING

'I'm often asked why I think the shop became a success considering that we opened just as we were coming out of the early nineties recession. I believe that it was because the brand's premise was so unexpected and unique compared with what was out there. It had a distinctive look that has become our signature.'

As a company that has never advertised, Cath Kidston has established itself as a very recognisable brand in a relatively short period of time. Today more than 50 per cent of British women (aged between sixteen and sixty-five) are aware of the Cath Kidston brand. For a business with a relatively small presence on the high street, this is a feat that many older, more established and more widely distributed brands would be happy to achieve.

'The signature look wasn't created overnight, but I think the building blocks were put in place within our first few years of trading. When I opened my first store it didn't look like anything else out there. You have to remember that we were just coming out of an era that had been pretty flashy, when it had been about big logos, and black and white minimalism, or brash Versace-esque prints and lots of gold. I wanted my store to feel much simpler and all the elements of how I presented the store, the products and the branding, needed to reflect this pared-down aesthetic.

'In contrast to what had gone before, I looked for a logo that felt friendly and personal but with a bit of a vintage feel. I drew something out, almost in my handwriting, and a designer then took my sketch and worked it into what we have today. It's hardly changed in all that time. I chose red for the logo colour as it stands out from almost any background.

COMING OUT OF AN ERA THAT HAD BEEN SO FLASHY, I WANTED MY STORE TO FEEL MUCH SIMPLER, WITH A PARED DOWN AESTHETIC

'Being consistent and not chopping and changing our signature colours and typeface was really important in order to build recognition and be easily identifiable – whether for a customer on the street looking for our store or for someone receiving one of our catalogues in the post. It's very easy for designers and marketers to become bored with things they are looking at constantly, to want to tweak and make changes to logos and colours. But you have to remember that your customers aren't looking at the brand day in day out and don't get bored by it in the same way. In fact this familiarity that has grown over the years is probably part of the charm for a lot of our customers.

'As a direct contrast to the logo-loving nineties' brands, I decided not to have my name emblazoned on the outside of our products. Instead, we stitched a label inside that read, "Specially Made for Cath Kidston". Firstly, I wanted to make sure that people understood that this was an original product that I had designed, not something I'd just bought off the shelf. Secondly, I believed that the products should be recognisable as Cath Kidston because of the originality in design or the use of print. I only relented and put a logo on the outside of our products when we began to sell properly

The combination of the red logo
and pale blue shop front has stayed
constant over the years.

to Japan. The Japanese clients insisted that it was necessary;
a badge that their customers required. I still made sure the
logos were never very big though!'

Marketers often talk about the four Ps: product, price,
place and promotion, when determining how to build a
brand. For Cath Kidston, the formula should be expanded
to include a fifth P for prints, as these have not only made
the products recognisable, they have become synonymous
with the brand, making it stand out from competitors and

I wanted our mail order parcels
to look like special presents.

imitators. 'We started out using lots of floral-based prints and most of our early PR was for floral print items. Gradually we added other designs, such as Spot and Star as well as scenic prints, such as Cowboy. Even though we've had a number of imitators over the years, I think a Cath Kidston product is still recognisable by the way the print is drawn (they are often still hand drawn), the use of fresh colour, and how the print is placed and used on a product. We've asked our customers if they can tell the difference between a real Cath Kidston print and a look-a-like one, and although people can't say exactly why they recognise our designs, they seem to instinctively respond to the integrity of our print.

'Our signature look is colourful, cheerful, witty, but never too fussy, too pretty or too twee. The look has to be modern and fresh. I didn't want to simply reproduce old-fashioned prints. It's the contemporary twist on a classic that brings an element of surprise. Our prints are also described as nostalgic because they evoke a sense of memory, especially from childhood. We have lots of customers who tell us that the products make them smile because of the memories that the brand triggers. That emotional connection we have with our customers, the ability to make them remember happy times, is one of the things I'm most proud of.'

The prints and products came together to form a brand identity when Cath met the photographer Pia Tryde. The two women collaborated on Cath's first book, *Vintage Style*, and immediately struck up a rapport. 'Pia really understood how I wanted to present the brand and got the wit and cheekiness I wanted to showcase in our photography. We worked on the book together followed by the company's first professionally designed catalogue, and we then went on to collaborate over a number of years, which helped to establish a visual handwriting for the brand. Through Pia's photographic style and imagery we created something that showed the brand's sense of humour. It's very British in many ways to demonstrate an ironic streak.

'I used some of the money from the Ikea prints to fund our first full-colour catalogue as I felt it was a form of advertising worth investing in. It was a great way to communicate the brand's personality as well as showcase the breadth of our product offer.

'Our range of bags has also had an important role to play in spreading the word. Bags were amongst the very early products I made. At the start, they were in simply made-up shapes in the vintage cotton fabric. But when I discovered oilcloth, I was able to introduce new shapes and sizes as the rigidity of the coated fabric allowed for more variety in design.

'Our bags have always been big sellers for us and these products being carried on the arms of thousands of women have been like roving billboards for the brand over the years. That's why designing our own carrier bag was so important to me. I selected a very durable plastic that was strong enough

BEING CONSISTENT WITH OUR SIGNATURE COLOURS AND TYPEFACE WAS REALLY IMPORTANT

COMING UP ROSES

Bags have sold more than anything
over the years and are a great
advertisement for the brand.

to be reused. I deliberately chose plastic as it felt modern and I think people would have expected us to use a paper, retro-style carrier. I always like to add an element of the unexpected.'

With no formal marketing training, Cath instinctively understood the importance of branding, PR and getting your product noticed. 'If I'm asked how to go about starting a business, I would always advise someone to think about the fundamental strength of their idea. It doesn't matter how much marketing you do, if the idea isn't original or unique enough, it just won't fly.

'When I opened the first shop I was convinced that there was a gap in the market, the timing was right and that my idea was different enough to have appeal. Looking back I was probably a bit ahead of my time and needed to be patient to let people catch up, but I always believed in the concept and didn't mind going against the grain.

THE IMPORTANT THING IS TO STAY TRUE TO YOUR ORIGINAL IDEA AND DON'T GET SIDE-TRACKED

'I knew prints would play a big role in creating our identity but I don't think I realised just how important they would be as part of the overall handwriting for the brand. We experimented in the early days and tried including a lot more plain fabrics in our range, to sit next to the prints, but the prints always outsold the plain products many times over, so even though I liked that look, our customers made their choice and they chose more prints.

'It's very interesting to see how relevant what I did back then still is today. I guess that's a testament to the strength of the original concept. It's important to stay true to your original idea and not get side-tracked if you want to build something that has longevity. I knew we'd got it right, that we'd created a brand, when a few years after we opened the shop a journalist from *The Times* wrote that something was "very Cath Kidston"!'

IDEAS & INSPIRATION

'I was always influenced by the prints and fresh colours of my childhood – my bedroom with its pale blue walls and striped rosebud curtains, the magnolia chintz in our playroom, my favourite Ribena coloured dress. Smell may bring back memories for some, but for me it's more likely to be a colour or a pattern.'

Cath's first prints were based on old, out-of-copyright designs that she tweaked with a fresh eye. It may have been just a case of recolouring the pattern, but these updates transformed the original. 'When I opened my first shop, I sold vintage fabric on the roll, but my first print design – Rose Bouquet – was for wallpaper. I was inspired by a piece of wallpaper I managed to retrieve from a derelict cottage in Wales. I knew the wife of the owner of the Sanderson wallpaper company and she redrew it for me. We've rescaled and recoloured that print so many times over the years and it's become a classic for us.

'Gill Hicks, who became my first full-time print designer, originally worked at the shop as my Saturday girl. She was a mature student at Chelsea College of Art and Design at the time and was able to redraw and recolour prints from

77

the scraps of fabric I gave her, cutting and pasting the design together. Very soon, I started developing my own prints. My drawing skills were fairly basic so I had to keep the design and colours pretty simple. It was quite some time until I bought Photoshop to help us with more complex patterns.'

Cath's designs drew on the prints and colours of her childhood, but there were other influences too. 'As a teenager I spent hours in places like Kensington Market, coveting all the patchwork Afghan and Indian dresses that were around at that time and picking up scraps of unusual fabric. My sister had an old Ikat coat with a beautiful red rose lining, so that Indian, slightly hippy thing became an influence, along with the neat, early block prints of Laura Ashley. Designers like Kenzo, with his exquisite colour sense and prints, were hugely influential, as was Fiorucci for its sense of fun. Working for the textile dealer Joss Graham, I came to appreciate everything from Javanase batik to Moroccan wall hangings. At McKinney Kidston, I bought and sold endless pairs of antique curtains and classic antique fabrics. And of course, car boot sales in the nineties were full of the most amazing treasures. By the time I started at Cath Kidston, I had squirrelled away quite a large collection of vintage prints.

I WANTED OUR PRINTS TO BE UNEXPECTED, FRESH AND COLOURFUL, WITH A REAL SENSE OF FUN

'The thing that has always intrigued me about print is how it travels. You can take something like a classic rose design and see it reinterpreted in so many ways. In England you might find a bunch of roses on chintz furnishing fabric; in China the roses would probably be printed on red with clashing pinks. They might be woven into a Turkish kilim with a black background, or used to decorate a piece of French porcelain. I loved the idea of taking all this global inspiration and reinterpreting it through English eyes.

'Once I began to design, all these ideas came in to play. There is nothing unusual about taking inspiration from an archival print, in fact many designers do, but the important thing for me was to give it my unique stamp. I wanted it be unexpected, fresh and colourful, with a real sense of fun. I love mixing up novelty prints and florals, throwing in unusual colour combinations. I wasn't trying to be the next Ralph Lauren or Laura Ashley. It had to be relevant for contemporary products – not simply a reproduction of the past.

'In the early days, I invested in opening screens for my own prints with fabric suppliers. I had to print each design in three colourways to make it affordable and I would often have to finalise my colour choices at the mill when the rollers were moving. You were given a certain amount of wastage at the beginning of a roll and then you were on the press. I didn't even have a colour printer at that time, let alone a CAD (computer-aided design) system. And even at the printers, colours didn't pop on screen in the way they do today, so I'd be under a lot of pressure to get the colour right in the moment. On one occasion I managed to get the pink version spot on and the blue was okay, but the green didn't work well at all. I had to live with the results and make the best of it. I really was winging it!'

Fresh inspiration for Cath's print designs came from her trips with Hugh to the United States. 'Whilst Hugh was

My dog, the ever-popular Stanley,
has been a constant source of
inspiration for me.

working I'd be out visiting antique fairs, thrift shops or craft markets. One of my early prints, Strawberry, was inspired by the placement prints on 1950s tablecloths. Perhaps it was all the time I spent in the States that got me thinking about a guns 'n' roses theme, and from here I got the connection to

cowboys. I went back home and Gill created the all-over repeat Cowboy pattern that we have reinterpreted many times and remains in our range today. The fact that we first used the pattern for adult products was the unexpected twist. I also like to combine prints that you wouldn't think would work together, to design prints as "friends". With Cowboy, we twinned a rose print called Gypsy and that was probably the first theme we created.'

Second-hand stores, old textile catalogues and travelling also generate new ideas. 'At Cath Kidston we don't use trend forecasting agencies or colour predictors or do the rounds of the fabric mills. We prefer to discover things for ourselves, so it remains a little leftfield. We don't want to be influenced by our competitors or, even worse, end up with the same look as them. People often wonder how a colour can be the colour of the season. It's because designers all use the same trend forecasters and visit the same fabric fairs. The fabric dealers will sell designs directly to design houses that they then have the rights to use. I've never wanted to work that way.'

Everything is about adding character, injecting an element of surprise to a classic print or subverting it with a touch of irony. 'Early on, I wanted to have a seaside-inspired print as I remembered them being very popular when I was growing up but I didn't want to have the usual, what I thought of as twee, dinky sailing boats. We designed a print that had all the elements you'd expect, like the little sailboats,

lighthouses, gulls and so on. But when you stop and look closely you'll notice that our version includes a cruise liner and an oil tanker! We've always liked to mix things up and throw in something unexpected. I'd take bed linen and use it to make little girls' dresses, because the cotton fabric was so lovely and soft to the touch. We'd juxtapose clashing patterns, prints and plains. We helped people be a little braver in their choices.'

For Cath, prints may have been one of the original starting points for her designs, but prints without a purpose don't interest her. 'From the very beginning I wasn't interested in making things just for decoration. Anything that made it into the range had to be useful – and we still use the same criteria today. The first products were basic but practical, but because of the prints they weren't boring. They needed to be fit for purpose. Today we make tents. I don't think anyone would buy a tent from us just because it looks pretty.

'My philosophy was that the useful everyday things that we all need, such as an ironing board cover or a tea towel, didn't have to be dull. When I started the shop the trend still seemed to be for serious, grown-up things. I like things to be fun and friendly so I decided to make products that were practical and cheery. We presented everything in a lighthearted way and I think this helped the brand stand out.

'I wanted to show a sense of fun – that British sense of humour, a little bit witty, a little bit tongue-in-cheek. My dog Stanley has featured on many of our most popular products over the years and I think it's probably only the British who would be so crazy about their animals.' Over time, this sense of fun combined with a touch of irony has become part of the Cath Kidston brand's DNA.

BRANCHING OUT

'When you think about it, it's not often that you double your business in one fell swoop. Taking the decision to open a second Cath Kidston store was probably one of my biggest steps and it made me very nervous. You wonder whether the success of the first shop was just a fluke, if you can replicate that again.'

In 1999, after six years of overseeing just one shop in West London, Cath decided to expand the business. 'A lot of customers were coming to Clarendon Cross from south of the river, so I decided to open a store in Elystan Street in Chelsea Green to save those regulars making the trip. The location had that villagey feel I love. Back then, the street was lined with small, local shops; there was still a fish shop, a butcher, a greengrocer. It had a great sense of community.

'As we continued to expand, to Fulham and then Marylebone and then Wimbledon, we always chose shops slightly off the main drag. We made that our deliberate strategy until quite recently, positioning our shops alongside other more quirky stores, as we felt this environment sat well with the brand.

Our first store designer, Andy Luckett,
worked his magic and created the stand
at Maison & Objet from kit furniture
on a shoestring budget.

'At this stage, I had no ambitions to open a chain. I remember one occasion, not long after the Chelsea Green store opened, getting a phonecall from a customer who was standing outside the shop, asking why it wasn't open. It turned out that the girl who ran the shop hadn't turned up because she was sick, but back then we didn't have the processes or procedures, let alone the numbers of staff, to be able to cope with anything out of the ordinary. When things like that happened, I'd worry that we'd taken on too much and found it quite stressful. Those early days with the two shops were probably the most stressful of all for me, as I was trying to buy vintage for both stores as well as develop the wholesale business.'

Fortunately, the appeal of Cath's signature look was gathering momentum. 'When we launched the first shop, florals and vintage prints were not at all fashionable, but I knew that my original concept was strong and it was a case of being patient and waiting. As the millennium turned, suddenly my idea and consumers' tastes were in synch and everyone wanted the modern vintage look. We were lucky to find ourselves leading the way.

'The financial boost that the Ikea deal gave us enabled me to take the business to a whole other level. To help grow the wholesale side, we decided to exhibit at the trade show Maison & Objet in Paris. Being in more good independent stores would enable us to reach a wider audience and establish the brand. The high-end Japanese boutiques were also starting to place increasingly large orders and Cath Kidston was becoming a cult label in Japan.

'With the Debenhams deal, I had been quite naive about what kind of money I should ask for. But by the time I worked with Ikea, I had met Elaine Ashton, Pia's agent, and she negotiated the print rights on my behalf. That was a big lesson for me, as I probably would have been grateful

to accept half the money we eventually received, so I asked Elaine to freelance for us on other projects and eventually she came to work for the company full time – and happily, she's still here.'

Offers to collaborate and to license the Cath Kidston name were now starting to present themselves on a regular basis as more and more companies picked up on the brand's potential. 'There were some collaborations that felt like a good fit, like Roberts Radio and Churchill China, but others were a little off the mark, to say the least. So I asked Elaine to help sort the good from the bad offers and to negotiate terms on my behalf. Cath Kidston underpants anyone?'

Cath could now afford to develop more of her own prints and introduced a range of now iconic designs, which included Classic Rose; Cowboy; Spot; Bubbles; and Boat. She began phasing out the vintage stock in favour of her own prints and products. 'Alongside the products we developed with our new licence partners, we were introducing new categories such as kids and babies. I'm not sure why it took me another ten years to figure out that doing a proper kids' range was a no brainer: Cath Kids – there's a clue in my name!'

By the early noughties, the company was growing fast, enabling Cath to step up the speed of product development and subsequently the company's rate of growth. With a staff of around twenty-five, plus store employees, the expansion had resulted in several office moves, each time to bigger premises. And Cath had moved her stock management from the basement at Clarendon Cross to a spacious warehouse in Somerset in order to cope with growing consumer demand.

To deal with the complexities of a rapidly growing business, internal structures and processes had to be put in place. 'Jody Kerr, who had been working in wholesale, went

<u>LICENCE OPPORTUNITIES</u>
<u>WE SAID NO TO</u>

Printed disposable nappies

A 'trendy' walking stick

Mobile phone battery

Printer cartridges

Mug and jar cleaner (!)

Toilet brush set and matching mug

All things electrical:

kettle, toaster, coffee machine,

ovens (AGA), fridges,

freezers, dishwashers,

washing machines, food mixers,

blenders, hair straighteners

and hair dryers

Kitchen towels

Microwaveable boots,

bottles and hot packs

Men's underwear

Marylebone was our biggest and most
expensive store and really showcased
the ever-growing range.

on maternity leave and came back as our first personnel manager. (Although the extent of HR back then was pretty much being a friendly ear and counselling the shop girls on boyfriend problems!) I was still responsible for creative and product development, store design, openings and all major decisions, but managing an ever-growing team of people was not my forte. And with logistics, production, finance, sales and merchandising to think about, I knew I wasn't the right person to be "team leader".

'Now we were no longer just a handful of people, we had to act more professionally. One casualty was a long-standing team member who just couldn't adjust his behaviour to the new ways. With more and more people in the office, he found it difficult to be respectful and basically keep his nose out of other people's business. In the end, I was left with no choice but to ban my dog Stanley from the office. He stole one too many Double Decker bars from out of people's bags and left a trail of evidence behind him as he rifled through their rubbish bins. So, he had to go. Sorry Stan, you're fired!'

We signed new licence partners, including Churchill China, Craig & Rose paint and Fulton Umbrellas.

TIME TO LET GO

'From 2002 onwards, the company was expanding fast. On top of that, more and more offers, collaborations and overseas partnership deals were being put on the table for my consideration. I was starting to feel out of my depth!'

Due to the lack of proper systems, small cracks started appearing in the business. 'We were still handling stock manually without any IT management systems and our inventory levels were getting out of hand – they just weren't visible. By 2002 we found ourselves with far too much stock, so we decided to open a sale shop in Fulham, as a way to clear a lot of excess product. And a friend introduced me to Bob Knowles, a retail operations expert who agreed to consult with us on IT solutions. Bob installed our first EPOS system and taught us about retail management software. It was a big leap from handwritten carbon paper receipts but I'd never wanted to invest half-heartedly in systems. Now the time was right, so we invested in computers and software for the office and shops. (We were then promptly broken into twice and each time the computers were stolen!)'

Although the business was making a profit, there were issues with the warehouse facility in Somerset. 'Orders were not being fulfilled properly or on time and stock wasn't being monitored. We were working with a third party distributor who ran our warehousing, order fulfilment and call centre, but the man in charge was tricky to work with. Bob promised to go down to Somerset to sort things out, but the night before leaving the poor man had a stroke and was unable to come back to work. I really missed his support and needless to say, the situation didn't improve. We knew things had got really bad when a customer complained because an empty can of Special Brew had been delivered in with her pyjama order!

'It's always hard as the founder to know when you need to release the reins and ask for help. On the one hand, it's your baby and naturally you're very protective, but on the other hand, you always wonder when you'll make a bad decision that could be the beginning of the end. The business was starting to feel like a burden – I wanted to be able to share some of the decisions with people who had more experience of growing a business than me.'

Right on cue, Cath's friend, the handbag designer Lulu Guinness, introduced her to a group of investors who were helping to grow her business. Fifty-two individuals had invested in Lulu Guinness and, two years later, the company was thriving. 'The group was led by New York-based CEO Michael Schultz, a veteran of the Urban Outfitters group in America. Michael had developed the wholesale strategy for Lulu Guinness and successfully grown the company. I wanted the help of experts. I think when you're self-taught, you always worry about when you might get found out.'

The investment group recognised the potential in Cath Kidston, both in terms of wholesale distribution growth and improved profitability driven by better margins. And in 2003, Cath sold a majority share to LGCK (Lulu Guinness Cath Kidston), the trading company set up to manage both companies. 'I think Michael and the board were almost

WHEN YOU'RE SELF-TAUGHT, YOU ALWAYS WORRY ABOUT WHEN YOU MIGHT GET FOUND OUT overwhelmed by the possibilities the brand presented and were convinced that the potential for growth would come from wholesale expansion as well as entering new markets.'

With Michael Shultz as chief executive, a fourth store swiftly opened in Marylebone: 'Our biggest shop to date and a step into the next league in terms of visibility and rent.' And the company started sourcing products in Asia, which improved margins considerably. 'I love the fact that we still manufacture some of our products in the UK, but we'd had bad experiences with British manufacturers going bust, and struggled to find the right skills to make our products here, so Asia was our only option. I had no experience there, but Michael introduced us to an agent in Hong Kong who could source handbags, wash bags and the more complex small accessories we were looking for.'

Plans to open in America also got underway. 'Michael was based in New York, but travelling to London once a month, spending a week divided between Cath Kidston and Lulu Guinness, so I guess it was only natural to him that we should open an office and stores in the States.' To look after the day-to-day running of the business in London, the board appointed a UK-based managing director, Jo Staveley, previously MD at LK Bennett, who would balance Michael's wholesale experience with her wealth of retail knowledge.

'Moving forward, my focus would be on the creative side of the business. I tried not to meddle or get too involved in daily operational matters. However, within months of Jo and me working together we were both questioning the direction the company was taking and the wisdom of having a New York-based CEO. With hindsight, I sensed that things were not right early on and knew far more than I gave myself credit for – gut instinct around your business is as good as any formal training.' The ambitious strategy the new board had put in place was to bring challenging times for Cath and the business.

GROWING PAINS

'It was probably a classic case of too much, too soon. The investors wanted to capitalise on the momentum of the brand and all the opportunities that were coming our way. But the infrastructure just wasn't there and we didn't understand the implications of our rapid expansion.'

2004 was a big year for Cath Kidston. On the retail side, there were now five London shops, plus concessions in Harvey Nichols and Selfridges and the first factory outlet store in Bicester Village, Oxfordshire (to help manage stock levels). Cath Kidston products were now in over 500 stockists worldwide. And that June, the business also opened in America, with a 2,500 square foot store in New York's SoHo, an office nearby, and a second store planned for Los Angeles.

'When I think back, it seems crazy that we believed we were ready for this. One moment we were operating a handful of shops, all in close proximity to one another in central London. The next we were bi-coastal, with a New York office to boot. We were shipping everything from our Somerset warehouse, which still held its own challenges, and the diversity of our range led to some interesting enquiries from US customs. Importing a Sheila's Maid wasn't easy! Wash bags were mistaken for hash bags (thanks to a typo); and we were once asked to prove the provenance of the chickens whose feathers were used to stuff our cushion pads!

'We had three members of staff just looking after customs. I should have known then that we were in over our heads and should bow out gracefully. But with so much activity, it was hard to keep your eye on the ball.

'On the creative side, we were also faced with new challenges. Seasonal products were introduced for the first time in 2004, which meant designing ranges for spring/summer and autumn/winter. It's standard industry practice, but the switch to seasonal merchandise is a big shift for any business. We didn't understand what an autumn/winter range from Cath Kidston should look like and the products were poorly received. It wasn't surprising as we'd made dark and gloomy prints, not the bright, cheerful look the brand is known for. We followed what we were told was a more commercial look rather than staying true to our own aesthetic.

THE DIVERSITY OF OUR RANGE LED TO SOME INTERESTING ENQUIRIES. IMPORTING A SHEILA'S MAID WASN'T EASY!

'To make matters worse, we had pushed up our prices to meet the new margins dictated by the wholesale model, but we were experiencing quality issues with some of the new products. We received an order of knickers that had no elastic, a range of jewellery that snapped almost as soon as you touched it and moneyboxes that fell apart. Oh, and an egg timer that only worked for one minute. It didn't rain but it poured!'

In spite of all this, the brand continued to grow. 'It was amazing how much we achieved in eighteen months – it certainly wasn't all doom and gloom. Not only had we started to source in Asia, we were now hitting minimum quantities, which meant we could improve our margins and produce more intricate designs. By growing the business, we created new jobs in head office and in retail as we opened more stores. Jo stepped up and started to improve our internal company structure, bringing in new talent to the business. And the office environment on a day-to-day basis was really buzzy.

'But although sales continued to be good, it was apparent to me that the new strategy was flawed and attempting to implement it was overstretching the company. It was tricky to design the American stores remotely. Even the difference of working in feet and inches rather than metric caused all sorts of issues. We had staffing problems too. One day, the LA shop didn't open because the shop assistant had gone off to an audition. And when we visited the LA store in 2005 it was really dirty and uncared for. The shops never took off in America and they closed in May 2007.

'Unfortunately, what was dividing us was far more than the Atlantic. I realised that the board and I had different visions. On paper it looked like the business was a great success and that we were making money. In reality, the US expansion had cost us more than the business had. I was still owed quite a lot of money from the deal with LGCK; on top of that, I discovered that money that had been put to one side for reinvestment had been spent and before we knew it we had a cash flow crisis on our hands. I had to put my own money back into the business to get us through.'

Dodgy product included knickers
with no elastic!

Cath went to the board to ask them to reconsider the strategy and make key managerial changes – both at CEO and chairman level. 'Luckily the strategy and our financial problems hadn't impacted negatively on consumer perception, but I could see us getting into dangerous territory. The board agreed that change had to happen. The company refinanced, Michael Schultz left and the UK-based Peter Higgins came in as chairman. It was a tough year, but fortunately the brand was tougher. And to my surprise, so was I. The experience taught me some valuable lessons. I learnt that my point of view was valid and I could argue it strongly in board meetings. And that the right fit between people and business is vital. For all the expertise and wealth of knowledge that had come into Cath Kidston, it just hadn't gelled.'

WHAT CATH LEARNT

Stay true to your idea

Learn to say no

Don't confuse a distraction
for an opportunity

Trust your gut

Don't worry about speaking up

Know what you don't know

Don't be afraid to ask for help

Good people are not always
the right people

You're more of a fighter than you think

Stay focused

Inside our cavernous New York store – at 2,500 square foot, it was about three times bigger than what we were used to in the UK.

BACK ON TRACK

'When I did Radio 4's *Desert Island Discs*, the song I chose over all the others was 'Always Look on the Bright Side of Life'. Although it may seem a bit of an odd choice, and would probably drive me mad eventually, I chose it because I love the sentiment. I think you have to be able to laugh, even in the face of adversity!'

After eighteen months of internal turmoil, the management team at Cath Kidston was ready to regroup. 'This was a pivotal time for the company, so we decided to concentrate on the things we knew we could do well.

'A quick cash injection was needed, so we held a clearance sale at Chelsea Town Hall with all the stock left over from our autumn/winter range. We had no idea how well it would go, but on the first morning I went off to buy everyone doughnuts from around the corner, and returned to see a queue stretching all the way along the street. Those Chelsea ladies went crazy when the doors opened! They were literally pushing each other aside to get to the stock. One woman even put her baby in one of the dog baskets we were selling so she'd have both hands free.

'Over two days we took £180,000. Customers queued for up to four hours just to get in. Everyone from the office pitched in, and Jo and I ended up with money stuffed everywhere – bags, pockets, even down our bras! It may not have been the most sophisticated event but it cleared a lot of stock – and helped our cash flow. It also gave me renewed confidence in the brand. Sometimes you just have to get practical.'

JO AND I ENDED UP WITH MONEY STUFFED EVERYWHERE – BAGS, POCKETS, EVEN DOWN OUR BRAS!

Back in the office, Cath's new role as creative director meant that she could focus on product design and development. 'We reviewed our pricing and margins to ensure that the products represented good value for money. We looked at quality standards to ensure the designs were true to the Cath Kidston aesthetic and the products weren't going to fall apart. Because we were sourcing more and more in Asia we could be adventurous with our designs and keep the prices down. The focus was all about giving the customers a good product at the right price.

'When you have the right people around you, work becomes a joy, and some strong characters emerged during this time. Peter Norris, who was on the board, became our Mr Fix It whenever we had a problem. We dubbed him the Godfather as he was the unofficial leader of the group of investors and a real lifeline during the tough times, and then when we were getting back on track. Mike France and Peter Ellis, formerly of the Early Learning Centre, were also great people to have on hand. They originally came into the office with a view to investing in the company. This didn't happen, but they became great sounding boards for Jo and me as we put together our recovery plan. ELC was another small, innovative business that had experienced rapid growth, so Mike and Pete had a valuable perspective to share.

'One of the significant adjustments we made was deciding to reduce the wholesale range of products and the number of wholesale doors, and renew our focus on the retail side of the business. We had found out the hard way that we weren't ready to expand in America, but there were still plenty of opportunities for us in the rest of the UK and in Japan, where we had a proven market. My early strategy had been to open stores in London, within a relatively small radius. It kept control and communication far simpler and meant that we were able to transfer stock and share staff easily if needs be. But Jo's retail experience gave her a sound knowledge of the UK property market and the company was now ready to move further afield.

'The first big test for the brand outside of London was opening a full-price store in Bath in 2005. We took the front section of an antiques market rather than a traditional shop unit. The rent was peanuts. It was also cheap to kit out as it still had all the old fittings.' Bath was followed by shop openings in Brighton, Bristol, Cheltenham, Edinburgh, Kingston, St Ives, Tunbridge Wells, York and a host of other places, bringing the total to thirty-five Cath Kidston shops and concessions in the UK and Ireland by the end of 2010.

Alongside this retail expansion, a series of high-profile collaborations helped heighten brand awareness and introduce the prints to a whole new audience. 'We joined other leading designers in decorating a Sky+ satellite box as part of a big promotional campaign. We decorated a Smart car for Selfridge's window. And we did something a little unexpected too.

'We've always been good at anticipating the next big thing and were amongst the first to pick up on the whole "glamping" and festival trend. In 2005, we launched a range of outdoor products, including a collaboration with the camping specialists Millets to do a tent. Some may have thought it an odd partnership, but it was so on trend. There was a great shot in *The Times* one weekend showing a sea of boring brown and green tents at Glastonbury and sticking out like a bright, flowery sore thumb was ours. You'd never get lost in a field with a Cath Kidston tent!'

The media interest continued with the company's successful collaboration with Nokia and the Carphone Warehouse in 2006. 'When you are approached and companies want to be associated with you, it's always a sign that the brand is hot. We were excited to put our prints on a range of mobile phones for the Carphone Warehouse. At

Exclusive Cath Kidston designs for over 40 simple sewing projects

that time Nokia was the biggest mobile phone company in the world and the designs were brilliantly advertised. Appearing in an ad break in the middle of *X Factor* Saturday evening TV was beyond what we'd ever imagined!'

Cath also branched out with a series of practical books, including *Make!*, *Sew!*, *Stitch!* and *Patch!*, featuring simple patterns and easy-to-make projects. 'It wasn't an obvious product category I guess, but sewing and crafting were such hot trends by the mid noughties and we were picking up on people's desire to make things for themselves or put in a little bit of effort to create unique gifts.' *Sew!* became the top selling craft book of all time in the UK (and has sold 325,000 copies worldwide) and all the books topped the craft bestsellers list.

'There's that great saying, "When you're in a hole, stop digging!" And that's precisely what we did by throwing ourselves into these new projects. We were fortunate that the brand was resilient but we had to turn things around quickly. So we stopped firefighting all the time and started planning for the future. If you're constantly reacting to problems, you can't move forward. But by making focused decisions, we smartened up our act. It was all part of growing up.'

T2

24.06.05

REPORTAGE
Should we
really be
so cruel to
celebrities? **4**

SOUNDS
■ Our guide to the best
and brightest bands
■ Plus: festival alternatives
■ Catching the Bach bug **9-16**
TV & RADIO 19-23

THE TIMES
FRIDAY

THE NEW GLASTONBURY
SOUNDS SPECIAL: Caitlin Moran, the music and the mood **INSIDE**

HEADING EAST

'With our new focus on growing the retail side of the business, we turned our attention to Japan, where Cath Kidston was already a cult label. We opened our first stand-alone store in the Daikanyama district of Tokyo in 2006. The new store was mobbed as soon as the doors opened. Needless to say, it was all very exciting.

'Right from the very early days, Japanese customers came to my first shop in West London. We had been selling really well in boutiques across Japan for years, so it made sense to build on the brand's cult status there. The plan was to grow organically, looking at various locations across Japan. And rather than run things from the UK, we partnered with a Japanese business called United Arrows and opened shops in key department stores – a very common practice in Japan. UA have an impressive record of taking European brands and establishing them in Japan, so we knew that this was a very different deal to the American expansion, and a move into the big league. But the day our first stand-alone store launched in Tokyo was still mind-blowing. We had crowds of people waiting outside. It's strange and very humbling to have security crowd control your opening!'

These days, Cath is treated like a celebrity whenever she visits Japan. 'The brand is so big there, sometimes I travel under a pseudonym in order to avoid attention. It amuses our assistant to think up funny code names for me and so on one trip, the person meeting me at Narita airport was asked to hold up a sign with "Barbara Windsor" written on it. But in a real lost in translation moment, the alias actually read "Barbar Windsor". I had that card in my office for quite some time!

'I have huge admiration for Japan and always find my visits inspirational. Our fans really get the Cath Kidston aesthetic, with its nod to nostalgia, quirky details and sense of fun. They collect items across the seasons and are so knowledgeable about the brand, it encourages us to try out new ideas. Like the mook (a uniquely Japanese magazine-book fusion). We sold over half a million copies of our first mook in Japan; our fifth, which we called *Hello from London*, sold over a million copies and we celebrated with a huge party at the British Embassy in Tokyo. The building looked spectacular with our Spray Flowers projected onto the facade. We were also thrilled to create our first ever Cath's Café, which serves cream tea and a traditional English breakfast, in Tsujido-Shonan, a seaside town in Kanagawa.'

By the end of 2010, eight Cath Kidston stores had opened in Japan and the potential for successful global expansion was becoming evident to industry observers. Despite a difficult market and global economic recession, the company saw pre-tax profits grow by 60 per cent in the year ending 29 March 2009. The shareholders who had bought in six years earlier were ready to sell up and Cath was happy to sell a further part of her stake in the company in order to move the business forward.

'We started talking to private equity investors with the expertise and international reach to take us to the next stage in our development.' In April 2010, TA Associates, one of the oldest and largest private equity companies in the world, bought a majority stake in the company. 'The original shareholders saw a very healthy return on their investments. I don't think that any of us who had lived through those tough times would have imagined seeing such a positive outcome.' The following year, Cath Kidston also signed a new partnership deal in Japan with Sanei International to roll out more stores and up the pace of expansion there.

In the first set of results after TA Associates acquired a majority stake in the company, sales climbed to £68.9m and the operating profit almost doubled in the fifty-three weeks to April 2011. 'Success hasn't just been confined to the UK and Japan, the company has made new partners across Asia, and there are now Cath Kidston shops in Taiwan, Korea, Hong Kong, Thailand and mainland China. In fact, there will be around fifty stores in Asia by the time this book is published!'

A book signing in one of our Tokyo stores.
The Japanese customers are so enthusiastic
– I can never quite believe how crazy it
gets on my visits.

COMING OF AGE

'Success is not a question of living in the past. We are always conscious of moving the product on, of keeping it current. Even with the idea of modern vintage, each generation has its own version of what that means. So I will often question if a particular item is relevant for the way we live today.

'For example, recently I've been wrestling with whether we should have egg cosies in the range. Does anyone actually use an egg cosy? When I look back at some of our old products, they are completely of their time – like the cover for the Apple iMac computer. It looks so enormous and dated when you compare it to the iPhone or iPad cases. But our designs are now bestsellers in the Apple stores. We make sure we progress by evolving themes over time and now we've built up a library of classic prints that we can draw from and constantly reinvent.'

The business still faces many challenges, of course. 'In some ways, I feel like the bigger the business, the bigger the challenge, especially when it comes to staying true to our core values as the brand grows and new people come into the company. We're becoming more knowledgeable about who our customers are and what they like and we need to understand how to use this information wisely. It makes sense to engage with our customers as much as possible and, corny as it might sound, people seem to value that connection. We get sent lots of photos of sewing projects and finished patterns from the books. The response to any craft events we run in our stores is phenomenal. Whether it's creating Christmas decorations or a make-your-own Stanley competition, people tell us they love to get involved.'

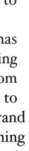

To ensure the business stays on track, Cath has produced a brand book, so that everyone working for the company can get to know the business from Cath's perspective. 'I realised that it was time to

restate what I'd imagined for the brand in the early days. It was an interesting coming of age exercise for me, as it made me appreciate that all the pieces that were part of my original idea twenty years ago are still relevant today. In fact, the closer we stay to those ideas, the better the product and the better the customer reaction. Ours isn't a bland corporate image and as we expand it's vital to retain our passion and integrity within the company in return for our customers' loyalty.

'Having a clear road map has enabled us to put the fun back into what we do. Stanley now has his own Facebook page and an email account to deal with all the fan mail he gets. I finally got the chance to go on *Blue Peter* and be awarded my *Blue Peter* badge! And in the summer of 2011, we bought an old library van, gave it a CK makeover and toured shows and festivals across the UK. Alongside Cath Kidston products, we offered all kinds of attractions, like face painting and mock tattoos, so the van proved quite a hit, and some weeks it even outsold a few of our permanent shops in terms of turnover!

Standing (centre) with the Blue Peter presenters
in front of my kitchen sponge village. I had to
go barefoot, so I wasn't a head taller than
everyone, but I was thrilled to appear on the
show and finally get my badge!

'One of the really positive things that comes with the company becoming more successful is being able to harnesss all that brand awareness and get involved with some great causes.' Over the past few years Cath Kidston has developed special products for various charities, including exclusive key rings for the homeless charity Shelter and a range of t-shirts and dresses for Uniqlo in association with a Japanese NGO, which is funding a safe motherhood programme in Zambia. 'One collaboration we were particularly proud of was designing an eco shopping bag for Tesco made from plastic drinks bottles. The bags saved millions of bottles from going into landfill sites and raised almost £500,000 for Marie Curie Cancer Care. It was a pretty big deal for us to be part of that.'

Cath Kidston head office now stretches over four floors of a modern office building in Shepherd's Bush, West London. It may not look much from the outside, but once through the doors you immediately enter CK world, the walls papered with floral prints, old repainted tables and chairs replacing the standard corporate decor, and vases of fake flowers everywhere. Cath's office has a sign on the door that reads 'Stan's office' and she still keeps a dog bed under her desk for the odd occasion when Stan is let through the door.

On the top floor is the boardroom, a Cath's Café (in place of a staff canteen), and a newly created "mock shop" – a replica Cath Kidston store with all the products for the season. 'The visual merchandising team gets to plan and mock up window campaigns. And all the different departments can get a feel for how their designs will come together on the high street.' The design area is now called 'the hub'. Scraps of fabrics and bits of inspiration are pinned onto boards around the walls: a doll's dress brought back from an antique fair; a tiny snippet of wool just the colour to accent a new bird print; a favourite t-shirt of Cath's to illustrate the perfect silhouette, and lots of ephemera gathered on inspiration trips.

'We've come a long way from it just being me and Gill designing everything. Now Design and Buying are split into specific category teams: Home, Accessories, Fashion and Kids, and each team has its own print designers, a head buyer and several assistant buyers. We have around 200 people in head office – specialising in everything from HR to Store Design to E-Commerce – and another 200 working full-time in our stores. I think the size of our new warehouse in Cambridgeshire brought home to me how big the company has grown. It's huge. You can see it from the motorway!'

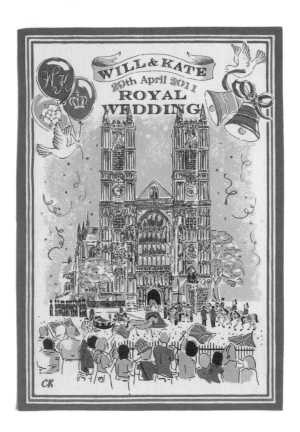

Unfortunately Kate didn't buy one
of the commemorative tea towels when she
popped into the Sloane Square store that
day, but we know she's a fan!

A ROSY FUTURE

'It's now twenty years since I opened my junk shop in Clarendon Cross. I never expected the business to grow the way it has. But looking back over the ups and downs, the thing that has kept me going is the endless opportunity I can see ahead. It's always been a case of taking a deep breath and moving on to the next level.

'A lot of people would say it's foolish not to have debt and that I grew slowly as a result, but I didn't set out to make a fortune. By ploughing profits back into the business, Cath Kidston became a long-term investment. We made changes, invested in our organisation, warehouses and supply chain, and improved customer service. That's why we're reaping the benefits today.

'In the past few years, the business has continued to grow in the UK. From being a very London-based brand we now have shops as far afield as Aberdeen, Jersey and Dublin. There are still towns where we'd like to be and it's just a question of time until we find the right locations. All the new stores we've opened recently have outstripped our expectations. We're also confident now that the brand can travel – it strikes a chord with consumers across the world, although I can't say whether that's down to the brand's sense of humour, its cheerfulness or the fact that we stand out from the crowd. But we're happy to tread carefully. For example, we've just opened shop in two El Corte Inglés department stores in Spain: we test the waters and enter new markets when we feel the time is right. After our experience in America, we won't overstretch ourselves again.

THE BEST LEGACY I CAN LEAVE IS THAT THE BRAND HAS LONGEVITY AND CAN SURVIVE BEYOND AND WITHOUT ME

'The team these days is a real mix of old experience and new talent. There's a real ebb and flow of people, with some leaving to have babies and some going to work elsewhere, then returning to us. We still have people who work for us who were with me from the early days, when we all shared the same office and had to turn our hand to whatever needed to get done. In fact, our longest standing employee, Mary, worked with me at Clarendon Cross and still works for us today part-time at the Portobello Road store.

'We respect the wealth of experience our long-term staff can offer. We've also brought in people with knowledge of running big businesses. A few people have come in with impressive CVs who didn't understand our core appeal, and those appointments didn't work out because they were making purely commercial decisions. It is so easy to damage a brand, but continued success will mean continuing to do things with real heart and soul. First and foremost we have to be about making a great product with great prints that our customers will love. It's too easy to chase commercial success at the expense of the values that have brought that success in the first place. But if there isn't true passion for what you do, it always shows.

'Maintaining the human side to how we do business is very important to me. Being mindful of the culture, of how we keep people within the business and retain our personality is key. I always said I wouldn't feel that I'd succeeded until we had two things: a proper restaurant for our staff, so they could get decent food at a good price during their working day, and a crèche. One down, one to go!'

Finally there is the question of how Cath fits into the changing picture. There is a long list of companies whose founder has exited soon after private equity has bought a stake in the business. For some founders a new direction, the loss of control or simply disliking the new regime is enough to make them walk away. It's happened with big fashion names like Jill Sander and Helmut Lang, and closer to home, with British businesswomen such as Jo Malone and Linda Bennett of LK Bennett.

'Sometimes it's a case of "don't mention the F word", as everybody knows that the "founder" can be a sensitive subject. But my ambition has always been for the business to reach its full potential and that means bringing in fresh ideas, new people and proper investment. For me the best legacy I can leave is that the brand has longevity and can survive beyond and without me.

'The business still feels like a family to me, with all its ups and downs, and I often use the parent/child analogy to try and describe my relationship towards it. As the parent, it's natural that you're needed and want to be needed in the early years as your child grows up. Then as the teenage years approach you have to let go a little and allow your child to stand on their own two feet. You offer help and guidance, but twenty years on, you want your child to be independent and not bringing their dirty washing back every weekend. You don't want to be at their beck and call all the time!

'I feel the same way about this business. I always want to be involved in some capacity, to offer a perspective, almost as the wise old owl. I'm enjoying work more than I have done in ages with new people like Paul Mason, our chairman and Kenny Wilson, our CEO, as they both understand how important it is for me to retain a family feeling within the company. But I will only know that I have done a good job if I manage to let go at some stage and allow the business to flourish without me.

'I have a number of really talented colleagues in the design department who will easily fill my shoes one day, but for someone who still works five days a week and loves it with a passion, stepping away will be hard. I never envisaged I'd make as much money as I have done from the business, and that's very nice, but it's not what makes me want to come to work each day. I always wanted to make a living and have fun. And I'm still enjoying myself too much to want to stop.

'I believe that what we've achieved so far is just the tip of the iceberg; I want to see what comes next! It will be interesting to see where we are in five years' time. I'm sure I won't be lying on a beach somewhere twiddling my thumbs, but I very much hope that I have made that leap of faith in the team. That's the target I've set myself over the next few years – it's going to be my toughest challenge yet!'

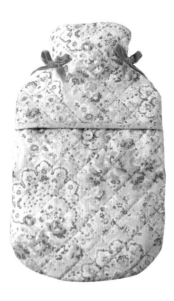

CATH'S DESERT ISLAND DISCS

The Rolling Stones:
Little Red Rooster
Louis Armstrong and Ella Fitzgerald:
Cheek to Cheek
Lou Reed:
Walk on the Wild Side
Bob Dylan:
I'll be your Baby Tonight
Spearhead:
Can't Let Go
Lucinda Williams:
There's a Hole in my Bucket
Phil Collins:
In the Air Tonight
Eric Idle (from Monty Python):
Always Look on the Bright Side of Life

Book

Larousse Unabridged
French Dictionary

Luxury Item

Hot water bottle

COMING UP ROSES

The publishers would like to thank the following for their permission to reproduce images in the book. We have made every effort to trace the photographers and copyright holders and apologise in advance for any unintentional omission. We would be pleased to insert the appropriate acknowledgement in any subsequent edition. Pages 2, 63 Pia Tryde/Ebury; 6 –7 Pia Tryde (Caravan design by Jo Sanders); 8, 54–55, 66, 70–71, 98, 102–103, 108, 112, 118, 133, 142 Pia Tryde; 10, 13, 15, 16, 19 Cath Kidston Personal Archive; 20 Jane Ashley; 23 Evening Standard/ Hulton Archive/Getty Images; 28–29 Fritz von der Schulenberg/© The World of Interiors; 31 John Hollingsworth/© The World of Interiors; 32 Christopher Simon Sykes/© The World of Interiors; 36–37, 38, 41, 42 –3, 46 Cath Kidston, Harriet Beauchamp, Sara Grain and Mark Schnell; 42–3, 49, 58, 60, 72, 76 Cath Kidston; 44, 45 (Swimsuit Design by Totty Whately), 64, 73, 74, 79, 81–96, 115, 121, 126, 132, 137, 138 Cath Kidston Ltd; 47 Andreas von Einsiedel; 48 © The World of Interiors; 50 © David Cumming/Eye Ubiquitous/Corbis; 56 Peter Aphrahamian; 65 IKEA; 69, 78, 100 Hugh Padgham; 80 Cath Kidston Ltd vintage archive; 104 Roberts Radio; 106 Kane Dowell for Cath Kidston Ltd; 107 (left) Churchill, (centre) Craig and Rose, (right) Fulton Umbrellas; 117 Jens Umbach; 121 Carphone Warehouse/Nokia; 122 Quadrille Publishing Ltd; 123 The Times/NI Syndication; 124 Claire Richardson; 127 Danielle O'Driscoll for Cath Kidston Ltd; 128–129 © Takarajimasha; 130 Cath Kidston Ltd/Thanks to all the entrants of the Make Your Own Stanley competition; 132 Venom Communications Ltd/Cath Kidston Ltd; 134 –135 Blue Peter/BBC/ Jessica Pemberton; 136 Barcroft Media; 144 Akemi Kurosaka